D1296952

COME HOLY SPIRIT

COME HOLY SPIRIT

Practical Prayer Services for Parish Meetings

ARCHDIOCESE OF DETROIT

AVE MARIA PRESS
Notre Dame, Indiana 46556

© 1994 by the Archdiocese of Detroit. All rights reserved. Published in 1996 by Ave Maria Press, Inc., Notre Dame, IN 46556

International Standard Book Number: 0-87793-592-0

Cover and text design by Katherine Robinson Coleman

Printed and bound in the United States of America.

Library of Congress Cataloging-in-Publication Data
Come Holy Spirit : practical prayer services for parish meetings / Archdiocese of Detroit.
        p.   cm.
    ISBN 0-87793-592-0
      1. Catholic Church—Prayer-books and devotions—English. 2. Church meetings—Prayer-books and devotions—English.
    I. Catholic Church.   Archdiocese of Detroit (Mich.)
BX2170.P32C65   1996
264', 0274—dc20   96-9294
                                                          CIP

ACKNOWLEDGMENTS

Many persons contributed to this project in many different ways. We wish to give special recognition to the following individuals for their generous time, energy, and careful thought that resulted in *Come Holy Spirit.*

Special mention is due Fr. Gerry Shirilla and James Kiefer who together envisioned the project.

The Prayer Service Composers

Michele Baines Angela Cerna-Plata, IHM Donald Clark

Norah Duncan IV Judith DuLong Elaine Eisenstein

Carol Gardner Joyce Jaxson Emelia Junk

Fannie Larkins Gloria Lewis Marie Markel, IHM

Michael McCallion Barbara Niemojewski Patricia O'Brien

Margaret O'Malley Daniel Rogozinski Stanley Stasko

Thomas Templin Marcia Woodward

Contributors and Project Oversight

Alfredo Aguirre Jr. (Project Coordinator)

James Kiefer

Stephanie Mitchem

Daniel McAfee

Department of Parish Life Director

Catherine Wagner

Contents

INTRODUCTION~11

How to Use These Prayer Services~12

SEPTEMBER~14

ONE   *Opening of the Year*~15

TWO   *Labor Day*~17

THREE   *New Work Begins*~20

OCTOBER~22

FOUR   *Change of Seasons*~23

FIVE   *Harvest Time*~26

SIX   *Month of the Rosary*~30

NOVEMBER~34

SEVEN   *Thanksgiving*~35

EIGHT   *Christ the King*~38

NINE   *Beginning of Advent*~40

DECEMBER~42

TEN   *Advent*~43

ELEVEN   *Christmas*~47

TWELVE   *Beginning of Winter*~50

JANUARY~52

THIRTEEN   *Beginning of the Calendar Year*~53

FOURTEEN   *Martin Luther King, Jr.*~56

FIFTEEN   *Prayer for Christian Unity*~59

FEBRUARY~62

SIXTEEN	*Lenten Promises~63*
SEVENTEEN	*Lenten Reconciliation~66*
EIGHTEEN	*Lenten Reflection~68*

MARCH~70

NINETEEN	*Prayer for Catechumens~71*
TWENTY	*Springtime~73*
TWENTY-ONE	*Easter~76*

APRIL~80

TWENTY-TWO	*Jesus Is Risen!~81*
TWENTY-THREE	*Easter Season~84*
TWENTY-FOUR	*Prayer for Neophytes~87*

MAY~90

TWENTY-FIVE	*Mary~91*
TWENTY-SIX	*Pentecost~94*
TWENTY-SEVEN	*Memorial Day~97*

JUNE~100

TWENTY-EIGHT	*God's Justice~101*
TWENTY-NINE	*Summer~105*
THIRTY	*End of the Year~108*

Introduction

$\mathcal{M}$eetings held by parish groups differ from business, civil, or neighborhood meetings in their call to prayer. Yet prayer on such occasions becomes staid if it is not prepared with some thought and care. But with parish groups made up of people coming from jobs, families, and other obligations, who has time to plan prayer well?

Come Holy Spirit addresses this important need for any group that meets at a parish. It includes thirty prayer services to be used over the course of ten months, from September to June, by the various groups that minister to and meet at a parish. These include—but are not limited to —parish councils, parish staffs, liturgy teams, adult education committees, school boards, school staffs, religious education directors and catechists, peace and social justice committees, and finance boards.

The services can be used at the beginning or end of a meeting or within the meeting itself. They reflect major events of the liturgical and calendar year. For each month, three selections are provided. This allows for use on a three-year cycle without repeating any service. Each prayer service provides plenty of ways to personalize and adapt its use according to the unique ministry and circum-stances of a particular group.

When prayer is done only by rote, it can become just one more item on the agenda. But for all in parish ministries, prayer is meant to provide mission and focus. *Come Holy Spirit* goes a long way to providing help to this end.

HOW TO USE THESE PRAYER SERVICES

Here are some tips for using the prayer services:

◆ Read through the prayer services. Select one to use for each month the group meets. Designate one person to be leader for each prayer service. Rotate this role so that the same one or two people are not always responsible.

◆ The leader's job is to read completely through a selected prayer service and make additions, deletions, or substitutions based on the resources at hand. For example, a suggestion may call for a paschal candle. The leader is free to substitute another type of candle if more easily accessible. The leader also assigns reading parts to other group members. For scripture readings, it is recommended that the leader provide the reader with the biblical texts beforehand so that the person has a chance to practice.

◆ Music is recommended for each prayer service and song suggestions based on the season or theme of the meeting are provided. The hymn books and publishers of the music suggested in this book are:

Gather, G.I.A. Publications, Chicago

Lead Me, Guide Me, G.I.A Publications, Chicago

Worship, G.I.A. Publications, Chicago

Cantemos al Señor (Spanish), Oregon Catholic Press, Portland

Canticos (Spanish), Oregon Catholic Press, Portland

Flor y Canto (Spanish), Oregon Catholic Press, Portland

Other music sources may be used. One group member functions as cantor with the sole purpose of beginning a song a cappella so that others may easily follow along.

◆ A bible or lectionary is always needed. A scripture reading is part of each prayer service.

September

ONE

*O*pening of the Year

COMMEMORATING OUR COMMON
AND INDIVIDUAL EFFORTS

An open bible (lectionary) and one large candle are placed on a table in the center of the circle. Each person takes an unlit taper, wax holder, and song book, and stands in a circle around the table.

 OPENING SONG

A cantor leads one of the following songs or another song that has been chosen.
"Sing a New Song to the Lord" *(Gather)*
"Lead Me, Guide Me" *(Lead Me, Guide Me)*
"Lord of All Hopefulness" *(Worship)*
"Quédate, Señor" *(Flor y Canto)*

Leader: As our parish ministry begins again, we call on God to send the Holy Spirit to guide us as we offer direction and support to our parish.

A period of silence is observed.

Almighty God,
we ask that your Holy Spirit open our hearts
that we might hear your voice in our lives
and continue to respond to your call with openness and
generosity.

Hear us, God, through Jesus Christ, our Lord.

All: **Amen.**

All are seated.

Reader: A reading from the first letter of Paul to the Corinthians.
1 Corinthians 3:9b-13, 16-17 (Lectionary, #704)

After a period of silent reflection, the leader, pastor, and some of the members of the group share brief thoughts and reflections on the meaning of the passage in light of the ministry of the group and its focus for the coming year.

The leader lights his or her candle and passes the flame around the circle until all the candles are lit.

Leader: God, your Spirit enflames our hearts. Come Holy Spirit, inspire our prayer.

Beginning with the leader, group members offer prayers of intercession which are both general in nature (e.g., for the whole church, world, etc.) and specific (e.g., for the group, the parish, personal intentions, etc.). The response is "Lord, hear our prayer" or "Come, Holy Spirit." After all the intercessions, the group stands and joins hands. The leader continues.

Leader: God, thank you for hearing our prayers. We offer them in the name of Jesus who taught us to pray: Our Father, who art in heaven. . . .

Let us offer each other a sign of peace.

The group members share a sign of peace using this form: "Peace be with you. And also with you."

 CLOSING SONG

A cantor leads one of the following songs or another song that has been chosen.
"This Little Light of Mine" *(Gather)*
"Blessed Assurance" *(Lead Me, Guide Me)*
"Father, We Thank Thee, Who Hast Planted" *(Worship)*
"Cantaré Alabanzas al Señor" *(Flor y Canto)*

TWO

Labor Day

COMMEMORATING OUR COMMON AND INDIVIDUAL EFFORTS

The group members gather and sit in a circle at a place other than where the regular meeting will be held. (An open space in the church sanctuary works well.) Song books are distributed. A fall or late summer flower arrangement provides decoration for the environment.

Leader: We gather in God's name to focus our thoughts on the inspirations of the summer months and the efforts that lie before us. Let us praise the Lord for the goodness we have been shown.

🌿 OPENING SONG

Song books are distributed. A cantor leads one of the following songs or another song that has been chosen.
"Come to the Water" *(Gather)*
"Here I Am, Lord" *(Lead Me, Guide Me)*
"Come, Ye Thankful People, Come" *(Worship)*
"Cánticos" *(Flor y Canto)*

Reader: In the building of God's reign, we are co-workers called to assist the Master Builder.

A reading from the first letter to the Corinthians.
1 Corinthians 3:5-17

A brief time of quiet reflection is observed. The leader then offers a commentary on the readings in words similar to the following, pausing between each question to hear from volunteers.

Leader: Saint Paul tells us that we are master builders, laying the foundation of God's kingdom. The foundation upon which we now build as part of our continuous efforts were first laid down by Jesus Christ and the apostles he chose. Our work today is a continuation of what was begun long before us.

In September, our nation observes a day in honor of those who labor. Labor Day is a reminder of the toil and effort that have gone into building our nation. What are some of the skills that have gone into building this nation that can be applied to the building of God's reign? These skills are many. How do they apply to our efforts as *NAME OF GROUP*?

After all who wish to share have done so, the leader asks that all stand and join hands.

The scriptures remind us that God's own Spirit guides our work. We need to remember that it is God who continues to plant the seeds among us that allow us to function and serve the needs of others in our parish. Filled with the Holy Spirit, let us acknowledge God's care and concern for us as we pray the words that Jesus taught us: Our Father, who art in heaven. . . .

The group members bow their heads. The leader extends his or her hands over them in prayer.

Leader: May the Lord bless us in all our works.

All: **Amen.**

Leader: May the Lord guide us in this coming year.

All: **Amen.**

Leader:	May the Lord help us to always serve our brother and sister parishioners in the ways of faith.
All:	**Amen.**
Leader:	May God bless us, in the name + of the Father, and the Son, and the Holy Spirit.
All:	**Amen.**

 CLOSING SONG

A cantor leads one of the following songs or another song that has been chosen.
"We Praise You" (*Gather*)
"Where We'll Never Grow Old" (*Lead Me, Guide Me*)
"O Christ the Great Foundation" (*Worship*)
"El Viñador" (*Flor y Canto*)

THREE

New Work Begins

BUILDING GOD'S REIGN AS
SUMMER ENDS AND AUTUMN APPROACHES

A bible (lectionary), lit candle, and crucifix are placed on a table in the center of the prayer space. The group members gather in silence and take a seat around the table. Song books are distributed.

Leader: God, we are called to a new year of service on behalf of our parish. Lead us and guide us on your behalf.

All: **Lord, send us your Spirit, and renew the face of the earth.**

 OPENING SONG

A cantor leads one of the following songs or another song that has been chosen.
"Come to Us, Creative Spirit" (*Gather*)
"Come We That Love the Lord" (*Lead Me, Guide Me*)
"O Christ the Great Foundation" (*Worship*)
"Espíritu Santo Ven" (*Flor y Canto*)

Leader: Let us pray.

Lord, we depend on you and the inspiration of your Spirit.
Help us to fulfill our mission as <u>NAME OF GROUP</u>.
Help us to respond generously to the needs of our parish.
Help us to listen to one another,
    to trust one another,
    to support one another.
Most importantly, in the midst of our work, help us
    to know you better.
We ask this through Christ our Lord.

All: **Amen.**

Reader 1:   A reading from the letter of Paul to the Ephesians.
Ephesians 4:1-7, 11-13 (Lectionary, #643)

*A period of reverential silence or a reflective instrumental selection
is offered as a response to the first reading.*

Reader 2:   A reading from the holy gospel according to Matthew.
Matthew 9:9-13 (Lectionary, #643)

*The leader mentions that the readings are taken from the feast day
of St. Matthew, September 21, and encourages group members to
share how their work for the coming year imitates Matthew's
action of leaving everything to follow Jesus and build God's reign.
The group members are reminded of last year's efforts, and asked
to share new insights gleaned from the summer that can help them
in the year ahead.*

*After a brief reflection time, the leader calls all to stand, join
hands, and recite the Our Father.*

Leader: God of goodness and blessing,
Guide our <u>*NAME OF GROUP*</u>
       to search out your Spirit among us.
Strengthen our resolve
       to do only what is good for our brother and sister
       parishioners.
May all of our efforts help to intensify your reign.
Let all see that you have called us to be your disciples in the
       building of your reign on earth.
Hear us, God, through Christ our Lord.

All: **Amen.**

 CLOSING SONG

*A cantor leads one of the following songs or another song that has
been chosen.*
"Now We Remain" *(Gather)*
"I Love the Lord" *(Lead Me, Guide Me)*
"Let All on Earth Their Voices Raise" *(Worship)*
"Vamos Cantantando al Señor" *(Flor y Canto)*

October

FOUR

Change of Seasons

OFFERING PRAISE FOR GOD'S GIFTS

The group members gather with song books in a circle of chairs, preferably away from the regular meeting tables or space. Decorative fall flower arrangements are a reminder of the season.

Leader: In the name + of the Father, and of the Son, and of the Holy Spirit.

All: **Amen.**

Leader: The grace of our Lord Jesus Christ, the love of God, and the unity of the Holy Spirit be with you all.

All: **And also with you.**

 OPENING SONG

A cantor leads one of the following songs or another song that has been chosen.
"Glory and Praise to Our God" *(Gather)*
"Joyful Joyful, We Adore You" *(Lead Me, Guide Me,)*
"This Day God Gives Me Strength" *(Worship)*
"Alabaré" *(Flor y Canto)*

Leader: All provident God, in your infinite love for us,
you provide all that is good.
May this autumn season help us to recall

the many gifts you have blessed us with
from your abundant harvest.
We ask this through your Son, Jesus Christ, our Lord.

All: **Amen.**

Reader: A reading from the book of the prophet Isaiah.
Isaiah 63:7-9 (Lectionary, #88.3)

*After the reading, the leader directs a shared reflection on its
meaning in relation to the mission and work of the group. After
the reflection, the leader begins the following intercessory prayer.
The response is "Lord, hear our prayer."*

Leader: For the gift of life, that we may protect and defend it in all
forms, especially in our own faith community, we pray . . .

Reader: For the gift of *NAME* our pope, *NAME* our bishop, *NAME* our
pastor, and all other leaders who help to guide and direct
our work, we pray . . .

For the gift of our families and friends who offer us their
support as we carry out this work, we pray . . .

For the gift of the communion of saints, especially members
of our own parish family who have died, who continue to
serve on our behalf, we pray . . .

For the gift of our natural environment, especially in this
local area, that continues to provide us with the resources
we need to live, we pray . . .

Leader: Heavenly Father,
these are but a few of the many gifts
through which we have been blessed.
We thank you for all that you have given us
through your Son Jesus Christ,
who lives and reigns with you and the Holy Spirit, one God
for ever and ever.

All: **Amen.**

The leader asks all to stand, join hands, and say together the Our Father.

Leader: As we continue to serve the needs of our parish, let us always be reminded of the many gifts that God has provided. May God continue to bless us in the name of + the Father, and of the Son, and of the Holy Spirit.

All: **Amen.**

CLOSING SONG

A cantor leads one of the following songs or another song that has been chosen.
"We Praise You" *(Gather)*
"Lead Me, Lord" *(Lead Me, Guide Me)*
"We Praise You, Father" *(Worship)*
"Cantaré Alabanzas al Señor" *(Flor y Canto)*

FIVE

Harvest Time

CALLING FORTH THE GIFTS OF THE FAITHFUL

A bible (lectionary), a bound notebook with blank pages, and a lit candle are placed on a table in the center of the prayer space. The group members take a song book and stand in a circle around the table.

OPENING SONG

A cantor leads one of the following songs or another song that has been chosen.
"Lift Up Your Hearts" (*Gather)*
"Great is Thy Faithfulness" (*Lead Me, Guide Me*)
"Pescador de Hombres" (*Lead Me, Guide Me*)
"Come, Ye Thankful People, Come" (*Worship*)

Leader: In the name + of the Father, and of the Son, and of the Holy Spirit.

All: **Amen.**

Leader: As we gather to serve the needs of our parish by providing leadership, guidance, and direction, let us pause and acknowledge God's presence in our midst.

Pause and allow time for quiet reflection.
Let us pray.
God our Father,
by the promise you made in the life, death, and resurrection

of Christ your Son,
you bring together in your Spirit, from all the nations,
a people to be your own.
Keep the church faithful to its mission:
may it be a leaven in the world,
renewing us in Christ,
and transforming us into your family.
We ask this through our Lord Jesus Christ, your Son,
who lives and reigns with you and the Holy Spirit,
one God for ever and ever.
(Sacramentary, Masses and Prayers for Various Needs and
Occasions, 1B)

All: **Amen.**

All are seated.

Reader: A reading from the first letter to the Corinthians.
1 Corinthians 12:4-11 (Lectionary, #67)

*After a brief period of silent reflection, the group chairperson rises
and offers a message in words similar to the following.*

Chairperson: During this season of harvest, we remember our own personal
gifts that we bring to this group. We have been especially
chosen to share these gifts with our brothers and sisters at
NAME OF PARISH. What are the unique gifts that *you* bring to
this group? I ask you to come forward one at a time and write
your name and a word or two that describe your gifts.

*Instrumental background music is played as the group members
come to the table one at a time, sign their names, and write a
description of their gifts in the notebook. When everyone has
signed the book, the chairperson holds up the notebook and
continues.*

In a spirit of good will and sacrifice, we offer these gifts to
the people of our parish. During this harvest time, when
nature offers its gifts to sustain and nourish the world,
may our gifts bring sustenance and nourishment to
NAME OF PARISH.

The group members may sit or stand for the following intercessions.
The response is "Lord, hear our prayer" or "Come, Lord Jesus."

Leader: Let us pray. May the gifts which God has granted us be harvested and be used well for this community of faith.

Reader: For the gift of cooperation so that we may better receive and bring support to one another, we pray . . .

For the gift of joyful hearts, that we may always experience the life of this parish in the light of the resurrection, we pray . . .

For the gift of love that we might see in every human being a brother or sister made in your image and likeness, we pray . . .

The leader calls others in the group to add personal intercessions.
When all intercessions are spoken, the leader continues.

Leader: God, hear our prayers and strengthen us.
In our common tasks, may we come to know your
        graciousness
and learn the importance of working together.
With your help, we offer the gifts you first gave us
in service of our parish.
May we also come to know in greater depths the peace
        and joy that
come in serving you through serving the needs of others.
We make this prayer in your name.

All: **Amen.**

The leader asks all to stand, join hands, and say together the Our
Father. The leader then extends his or her hands for a blessing.

Leader: Bow your heads and pray for God's blessing.
Always be near us, loving God.

All: **Amen.**

Leader: May Jesus be our way, our truth, and our life.

All: **Amen.**

Leader: May the Holy Spirit guide us on our journey.

All: **Amen.**

Leader: And may almighty God bless us in the name + of the Father, and of the Son, and of the Holy Spirit.

All: **Amen.**

CLOSING SONG

A cantor leads one of the following songs or another song that has been chosen.
"Sing to the Mountains" (*Gather*)
"We Give You Thanks" (*Lead Me, Guide Me*)
"Praise and Thanksgiving" (*Worship*)
"Cancíon del Testigo" (*Flor y Canto*)

SIX

*M*onth of the Rosary

LOOKING TO MARY FOR INSPIRATION AND PRAYERFUL INTERCESSION

A bible (lectionary), lit candle, rosary beads, and statue of Mary are placed on a table in the center of the prayer space. The group members gather with song books and stand around the table.

Leader: In communion with Mary, the Mother of God, and all the saints of heaven and earth, we begin in the name + of the Father, and of the Son, and of the Holy Spirit.

All: **Amen.**

 OPENING SONG

A cantor leads one of the following songs or another song that has been chosen.
"All Who Claim the Father of Jesus" (*Gather*)
"Sing of Mary" (*Lead Me, Guide Me*)
"Madre Oyeme" (*Flor y Canto*)

Leader: Let us pray.
Loving God, through the power of your Spirit
Mary became the mother of your Son.
She provides us, too, with a mother's care.
May our voices be joined with Mary

and all the saints in heaven
to bring you praise and glory,
now and forever.

All: **Amen.**

Reader: A reading from the holy gospel according to Luke.
                 Luke 1:26-38 (Lectionary, #712.3)

                 *The group members sit and observe a few minutes of silent or
                 shared reflection. Following the reflection, the leader introduces a
                 communal recitation of one mystery of the rosary.*

Leader: Mary, our mother, has been a model of prayer and of
                 intercession for us. She teaches us how to pray and she
                 prays for us as one who is most favored before God.

                 Our devotion to Mary strengthens our own faith. Her
                 support and prayers encourage us to share God's love with
                 one another. In this month dedicated to the praying of the
                 rosary, let us pray together one decade of the rosary,
                 reflecting on one of the holy mysteries.

                 *The leader announces the mystery. One person is designated to
                 lead the openings of the Our Father, Glory Be, and Hail Mary as
                 the rest of the group concludes each prayer. After the recitation,
                 the leader continues.*

                 Mary inspires us to prayer and good works. She is the
                 model of selfless giving. Let us pray together the traditional
                 Memorare:

All: Remember, O most gracious Virgin Mary,
                 that never was it known
                 that anyone who fled to your protection,
                 implored your help,
                 or sought your intercession
                 was left unaided.
                 Inspired by this confidence,
                 I fly unto you,
                 O Virgin of virgin, my mother.

To you I come, before you I stand,
sinful and sorrowful.
O Mother of the Word incarnate,
despise not my petitions,
but in your mercy hear and answer me. Amen.

Leader: God, thank you for hearing our prayers through the intercession of our mother Mary. We offer them in the name of Jesus who taught us to pray: Our Father, who art in heaven. . . .

Let us offer each other a sign of peace.

The group members share a sign of peace using this form: "Peace be with you. And also with you."

 CLOSING SONG

A cantor leads one of the following songs or another song that has been chosen.
"Canticle of Mary—My Soul Gives Glory" (*Gather*)
"Santa Mariá Del Camino" (*Flor y Canto*)

November

SEVEN

Thanksgiving

OFFERING OURSELVES IN A
SPIRIT OF GRATEFULNESS

A lit paschal candle stands in a prominent place near an empty basket. The chairs are arranged in a circle. A pen, a lap pad, and a sheet of blank paper are placed near each chair. The group members gather with song books and stand for the opening song.

OPENING SONG

A cantor leads one of the following songs or another song that has been chosen.
"Psalm 63: In the Shadow of Your Wings" (*Gather*)
"All Things Bright and Beautiful" (*Worship*)
"I Just Came to Praise the Lord" (*Lead Me, Guide Me*)

Leader: As our nation pauses to offer thanks, we, the members of
            <u>NAME OF GROUP</u> offer our gratefulness on behalf of our
            many blessings and the blessings of this parish.
            Let us pray.
            Lord, we have gathered in your name that we may do your
            will through the sharing of our gifts.
            Help us to be responsive and responsible.
            Help us to appreciate the gifts of others.
            Help us to grow in unity through the richness of our
                 diversity.
            May we always respond to your grace and be mindful of

our commitment as members of this group and parish. We make this prayer through Christ our Risen Lord.

All: **Amen.**

All are seated. The leader reads the following introduction, pausing between each question.

Leader: Please take up the lap pad, pen, and paper you will find near your chair. As you listen to the words of St. Paul to the church at Ephesus, reflect on the gifts of this parish community. What are the gifts that we are stewards of here? How can we better steward our gifts? How can we better nourish the talents of those who are present in our group? What challenges do we face in being stewards? For what are we most grateful as a parish? Jot down words or short phrases that come to mind as the reader pauses between scripture passages.

Reader: A reading from the letter to the Ephesians. (adapted from Ephesians 4)

I plead with you to live a life worthy of the calling received, with perfect humility, meekness and patience, bearing with one another lovingly . . .

The reader pauses to allow for reflection and writing.

Make every effort to preserve the unity which has the Spirit as its origin and peace as its binding force. There is one Lord, one faith, one baptism, one God and Father of all, who is over all and works through all and is in all. Each of us has received a special gift in proportion to what Christ has given . . .

The reader pauses to allow for reflection and writing.

It was Christ who gave apostles, prophets, evangelists and teachers in roles of service for the faithful to build up the body of Christ, till we become one in faith and in the knowledge of God's Son, and form that perfect one who is Christ. Let us be children no longer, rather let us live the truth in love and grow to the full maturity of Christ. Through Christ the whole body grows and builds itself up in love.

The group members reflect and write. Beginning with the leader, group members go around the circle sharing some of the reflections they have written. After each person has shared, he or she places his paper in the basket.

Leader: Dear God, in this season of thanksgiving, we have reflected on your word. We have been called to your service and we have answered "yes" to your call. We offer you our prayers, talents, and commitments in a spirit of gratefulness. Let your light and love guide our actions as we continue to draw meaning from our inspirations and live our resolutions. Draw us closer to you and to one another through the power of your Spirit.

All: **Amen.**

 CLOSING SONG

A cantor leads one of the following songs or another song that has been chosen.
"The Lord is My Life" (*Gather*)
"Let There Be Light" (*Worship*)
"Let the Heaven Light Shine on Me" (*Lead Me, Guide Me*)
"Gracias Señor" (*Flor y Canto*)

EIGHT

*C*hrist the King

INITIATING A KINGDOM
OF JUSTICE AND PEACE

A bible (lectionary), lit candle, and globe are placed on a table in the center of the prayer space. The group members gather in silence and stand around the table.

 ## OPENING SONG

Song books are distributed. A cantor leads one of the following songs or another song that has been chosen.
"Prayer for Peace" (*Gather*)
"I've Got Peace Like a River" (*Lead Me, Guide Me*)
"Shall We Gather at the River" (*Lead Me, Guide Me*)
"All Glory, Laud and Honor" (*Worship*)
"To Jesus Christ, Our Sovereign King" (*Worship*)
"Tú Reinarás" (*Flor y Canto*)

Leader: Gracious God,
you have called us to your reign under Christ our King.
Help *NAME OF THE GROUP* to be bearers of justice and a source of peace.
Remove all that may hinder our sight so that we may see that all people are equal in your eyes.
Send us your Spirit, Lord,
and make us instruments of your will.
We ask this through Christ our Lord.

All: **Amen.**

The group members take a seat.

Reader: A reading from the book of the prophet Isaiah.
Isaiah 9:1-6 (Lectionary, #14)
or
A reading from the letter to the Colossians.
Colossians 3:12-17 (Lectionary, #440)

Leader: Please reflect quietly on this question: How does our group reflect Christ's peace and how can we bring Christ's peace to others?

After a few minutes of quiet reflection, the leader calls on group members to share their reflections aloud. After the sharing, the leader continues.

Jesus calls us to be peacemakers, to give witness to the peace which only the Holy Spirit can bring. In the words the Lord taught us, let us pray: Our Father, who art in heaven . . .
As Christ brought peace to the world, let us offer each other a sign of peace.

The group members share a sign of peace using this form: "Peace be with you. And also with you."

 CLOSING SONG

A cantor leads one of the following songs or another song that has been chosen.
"How Can I Keep from Singing" (*Gather*)
"The Voice of God Speaks but of Peace" (*Gather*)
"Blessed Quietness" (*Lead Me, Guide Me*)
"Bless His Holy Name" (*Lead Me, Guide Me*)
"The King of Glory" (*Worship*)
"This is the Feast of Victory" (*Worship*)
"Oración de San Francisco" (*Cantemos al Señor*)

NINE

Beginning of Advent

PREPARING FOR THE COMING OF CHRIST

An Advent wreath with a single lit candle is placed on a table in one corner of the room. The rest of the room is darkened as the group members stand together on the opposite side of the room. There is no opening song.

Leader: The signs of Advent are upon us. Soon we will intensify our waiting for the coming of the Lord.

Let us pray.
Father in heaven,
our hearts desire the warmth of your love
and our minds are searching for the light of your Word.
Increase our longing for Christ the Savior
and give us the strength to grow in love,
that the dawn of his coming
may find us rejoicing in his presence
and welcoming the light of his truth.
We ask this in the name of Jesus the Lord.
(Sacramentary, First Sunday of Advent)

All: **Amen.**

All sit for the reading.

Reader: A reading from the holy gospel according to Mark.
Mark 13:33-37 (Lectionary, #2)

or
A reading from the holy gospel according to Matthew.
Matthew 24:37-44 (Lectionary, #1)

A brief period of silent reflection follows. After two or three minutes, the leader addresses the group, saying something like the following.

As Advent approaches, we focus our thoughts on Christ's coming. As <u>NAME OF GROUP</u> and as individual members of our parish community, what are we *expecting* from Christ? How can Christ's coming make us more effective individuals and members of this group?

Pause to allow volunteers to share.

Leader: Let us pray.

God of all our longing,
we bring before you the expectations and joys of our hearts.
As we begin this Advent season
may we live in hope,
journey in faith,
and strive to be leaders in this community.
Inspire us to be your faithful followers
as we carry on your work in this parish.
We ask this in the name of Jesus Christ.

All: **Amen.**

 CLOSING SONG

A cantor leads one of the following songs or another song that has been chosen.
"My Soul in Stillness Waits" (*Gather*)
"Psalm 146—Lord Come and Save Us" (*Gather*)
"Remember Your Mercy, Lord" (*Gather*)
"The King Shall Come" (*Lead Me, Guide Me*)
"O Lord of Light, Who Made the Stars" (*Lead Me, Guide Me*)
"Take Comfort, God's People" (*Worship*)
"King of Glory" (*Worship*)
"Ven Señor, No Tardes" (*Cantemos Al Señor*)
"Oh Ven, O Ven Emanuel" (*Flor y Canto*)

December

TEN

*A*dvent

SEARCHING FOR THE LORD

A bible (lectionary) and four candles of different sizes are placed on a table. Surrounding the candles are a miniature Santa Claus, a clock, a holiday bow, and Christmas lights. Chairs form a circle around the table. The group members sit for the opening of the prayer. Song books are distributed.

Leader 1:   How do we prepare for a gift that we have already received? God's love has already been poured out in the birth, life, death, and resurrection of Jesus. We await the One who is already here among us.

Leader 2:   As we move closer to Christmas
our shopping is more frenzied,
our bodies are more worn and wearied,
our energy is fading,
and our tempers begin to flare!

We ask:
Do I really have time for this meeting?
Let us use this time to accomplish something meaningful.
Let us slow down now as we contemplate Jesus' presence.

 OPENING SONG

A cantor leads one of the following songs or another song that has been chosen.
"Prepare Ye the Way of the Lord" (*Lead Me, Guide Me*)

"People Look East" (*Worship*)
"O Day of Peace" (*Worship*)
"O Ven, Oh Ven Emmanuel" (*Flor y Canto*)

Leader 1 leads a prayer dialogue. The response to each stanza is "May God fill our waiting hearts with Advent hope."

Leader 1:   Peace be with you, Servants of the Lord! May God fill our waiting hearts with Advent hope.

All: **May God fill our waiting hearts with Advent hope.**

Leader 1:   Lord, God, we give you thanks and praise
for you are our source of life and hope.
As we await the coming of Jesus in history,
create in us a desire to let Jesus be born anew in our hearts each day.

All: **May God fill our waiting hearts with Advent hope.**

Leader 1:   Alleluia! Prepare the way of the Lord;
make straight his paths;
all people shall see the salvation of our God.

All: **May God fill our waiting hearts with Advent hope.**

The group members stand for the reading of the gospel.

Reader: A reading from the holy gospel according to Luke.
Luke 1:67-79 (Lectionary, #201)

After the reading, the two leaders stand near the table. Leader 2 continues, holding the clock.

Leader 2:   Do we control time or does it control us? We are blitzed by the message that only scant few shopping days remain until Christmas.

Leader 2 places the clock under the table. Leader 1 continues, holding the Christmas lights.

Leader 1:   Twinkling lights and mall decorations create a shopping mood that taps our purchasing power.

Leader 1 places the lights under the table. Leader 2 continues, holding the Christmas bow.

Leader 2: Wrappings and trappings clutter our homes and our minds with everything but Advent hope.

Leader 2 places the box under the table. Leader 1 continues, holding the toy Santa.

Leader 1: Are our children waiting more anxiously for Santa then for Jesus? Are *we*?

Leader 1 places the toy Santa under the table. Leader 2 continues.

Leader 2: Let us pray.
Almighty and eternal God, you gave us time and space in which to build your kingdom.
As we prepare for Christmas, may our lives be guided by the timeless love of Christ.

Leader 2 lights one of the candles and continues. The group members respond to each stanza, "Come, Lord Jesus."

We light this candle of timeless love.
God of enlightenment,
may our vision be graced with the power to see
each twinkling light as an expression of Christ's body,
living in many parts in our midst.
We pray . . .

All: **Come, Lord Jesus.**

Leader 1 lights a second candle and continues.

Leader 1: We light this candle of enlightenment.
God, creator of the beautiful and eternal,
grant us the joy of discovering what is inside
our own packaging
and the wisdom to know that the love we give
is life's greatest treasure. We pray . . .

All: **Come, Lord Jesus.**

Leader 2 lights a third candle and continues.

Leader 2:   We light the candle of eternal treasures.
Almighty God,
giver of the greatest gift of all,
may the gifts that we give to others
express our far-reaching love. We pray . . .

All: **Come, Lord Jesus.**

Leader 1 lights the fourth candle and continues.

Leader 1:   We light the candle of God's generous, unconditional love.
Please offer your personal petitions
for this group, your family, or yourself.
Our response to each petition
will continue to be "Come, Lord Jesus."

After the sharing of petitions, Leader 1 leads a recitation or singing of the Our Father. Leader 2 then continues.

Leader 2:   All powerful creator of new life,
bring forth new life and hope in us.
May we continue to see you in the Christmas signs
around us
and make this a time of welcoming for Jesus to
be born in our hearts.

All: **Amen.**

 CLOSING SONG

A cantor leads one of the following songs or another song that has been chosen.
"Be Strong" (*Lead Me, Guide Me*)
"Soon and Very Soon" (*Lead Me, Guide Me*)
"God of All People" (*Gather*)
"Maranatha" (*Gather*)
"Ven, Señor, No Tardes" (*Cantemos al Señor*)

ELEVEN

Christmas

GIVING ALL GLORY TO
GOD IN THE HIGHEST

A bible (lectionary), large lit candle, and wreath are placed on a table in the center of the room. The group members take an unlit taper with wax holder, stand, and form a circle around the table. Song books are distributed:

Leader: Glory to God in the highest.

All: **And peace to his people on earth!**

 OPENING SONG

A cantor leads one of the following songs or another song that has been chosen.
"Glory to God in the Highest" *(a version familiar to the group)*
"Song of God Among Us" *(Gather)*
"Venid Fieles Todos" *(Flor y Canto)*

Leader: We give you praise, generous Creator God,
for you have filled the earth with signs of your love.
From the beginning of creation
you have made known your care for us.
In the fullness of time you sent us Jesus
to live and grow among us as a human being.
Through him you showed us how to live.

Through him you gifted us with eternal life.
As members of *NAME OF THE GROUP* OR *NAME OF THE PARISH,* we celebrate and rejoice in the gift of eternal life.
Hear our prayers of thanks and praise in Jesus' name.

All: **Amen.**

The cantor than leads the group members in singing an "Alleluia" in an arragement that is familiar to all.

Reader: A reading from the holy gospel according to Luke.
Luke 2:15-20 (Lectionary, #15)

All are seated. After a brief time for quiet reflection, the leader continues with the following litany. The response to each statement is "He is Emmanuel, God is with us!"

Leader: We celebrate the birth of Jesus, born for us as the anointed one of God . . .

All: **He is Emmanuel, God is with us!**

Leader: We celebrate the birth of Jesus, who in human life revered his heritage and his ancestry . . .

All: **He is Emmanuel, God is with us!**

Leader: We celebrate the birth of Jesus who prayed with his brothers and sisters and spent long hours in communion with God . . .

All: **He is Emmanuel, God is with us!**

Leader: We celebrate the birth of Jesus who preached God's Word and sought God's will with courage . . .

All: **He is Emmanuel, God is with us!**

Leader: We celebrate the birth of Jesus who sees our needs and constantly responds to them . . .

All: **He is Emmanuel, God is with us!**

Leader:	We celebrate the birth of one who lived, died, and rose to heaven for us. Jesus is God's gift to us. Let us reflect on some of the individual gifts present in our group. Please share a gift you have observed in someone else. It can be anything we have to offer: gifts of organization, gifts of communication skills, gifts of good listening, or gifts of reconciling. After you have shared, light your own taper.

The sharing and lighting of candles continues until all are lit. The leader then continues.

Leader:	Eternal God, you gifted us with Jesus Christ and we now share in your eternal life. You have sent the Holy Spirit to live among us. It is this same Spirit that calls us to this ministry. We ask your blessing on our gifts and on the work we do. We offer this prayer in Jesus' name.
All:	**Amen.**

CLOSING SONG

A cantor leads one of the following songs or another song that has been chosen.
"Joy to the World" or "Silent Night"
"Bring Forth the Kingdom" (*Gather*)
"Born of Peace" (*Gather*)
"Noche de Paz" (*Flor y Canto*)

TWELVE

Beginning of Winter

BRINGING OUR LIGHT
TO A WORLD OF DARKNESS

The participants enter the prayer space quietly and take seats. A flask of oil for anointing is placed on a side table.

 OPENING SONG

Song books are distributed. A cantor leads one of the following songs or another song that has been chosen.
"Here I Am Lord" (*Gather*)
"Night of Silence" (*Gather*)
"Lord, You Give the Great Commission" (*Worship*)
"Qué Bueno Es Mi Señor" (*Flor y Canto*)

After the song, the leader continues with the following litany. The response is "Help us to bring your light to the world."

Leader:	The Lord of dark, long, winter nights is with us.
All:	**Help us to bring your light to the world.**
Leader:	The Lord of cold and blustery storms is with us.
All:	**Help us to bring your light to the world.**
Leader:	The Lord of sleet and snow-filled skies is with us.
All:	**Help us to bring your light to the world.**
Leader:	The Lord of overcast and rain and wind is with us.

All: **Help us to bring your light to the world.**

Leader: All praise and thanks to you almighty God.
We gather in the name of our Lord and brother, Jesus,
as servants of your people.
We bless you for the coldness of winter that creates in us
an appreciation of the warmth of your love.
Grant that the light of your wisdom
may help us appreciate your presence with us.
Hear our prayer in the name of Jesus Christ, the Lord.

All: **Amen.**

Reader: A reading from the letter to the Ephesians.
Ephesians 4:1-6 (Lectionary, # 111)
or
Ephesians 5:8-14 (Lectionary, #31)

*After the reading, instrumental background music is played. The
leader asks the group members to come to the table in pairs to
anoint each other's hands with oil. The group members recite the
following prayer to one another as they anoint each other's hands:
"May this oil be a reminder that you are anointed to serve God's
people." After all have been anointed, the leader continues.*

Leader: Lord God,
in baptism we have been anointed and made holy.
Send us forth in the light of Christ
to bring light to a world of darkness.
We ask this in the name of Jesus, our Lord and brother.

All: **Amen.**

 CLOSING SONG

*A cantor leads one of the following songs or another song that has
been chosen.*
"We Are Called" (*Gather*)
"He Has Anointed Me" (*Gather*)
"Pescador de Hombres" (*Flor y Canto*)

January

$\mathcal{B}$eginning of the Calendar Year

BLESSINGS FOR GOD'S PEOPLE

The group members enter the prayer space and stand in a circle. Song books are distributed. Several different sizes and tones of bells are distributed to people in the group. The leader motions for a ringing of bells to begin the prayer.

Leader: Wonderful are your works, O Lord, and mighty are your deeds. As we begin this new year, we give you praise and ask you for your mercy, through Christ our Lord.

All: **Amen.**

 OPENING SONG

A cantor leads one of the following songs or another song that has been chosen.
"The Awakening" (*Lead Me, Guide Me*)
"God Has Smiled on Me" (*Lead Me, Guide Me*)
"All People That on Earth Do Dwell" (*Worship*)

After the song, the bell ringers ring a chorus of bell sounds before collecting the bells in one place. All are seated.

Reader:	A reading from the book of Genesis. Genesis 1:14-18 (Lectionary, #841) or A reading from the letter to the Colossians. Colossians 1:15-20 (Lectionary, #106)
	After a few minutes of silent reflection, the leader offers several prayers of intercession. The response is "Blessed be God forever."
Leader:	For the gift of new beginnings as we start a new year, we pray . . .
All:	**Blessed be God forever.**
Leader:	For the freedom of nations and the release of the imprisoned, we pray . . .
All:	**Blessed be God forever.**
Leader:	For all leaders in the church, especially *LIST NAMES OF LEADERS*, we pray . . .
All:	**Blessed be God forever.**
Leader:	For all from our parish, who are preparing for Christian initiation , we pray . . .
All:	**Blessed be God forever.**
Leader:	For the members of this group, that the new year may help us to accomplish all of our plans in God's name, we pray . . .
All:	**Blessed be God forever.**
	The group members are invited to share their own personal petitions. After the sharing, the leader continues.
Leader:	Loving God, everything we have comes from you: all peoples, all creation is yours. Watch over the lives of those gathered here. Help us to shape our lives according to your will. We ask this through Christ our Lord.

All: **Amen.**

Leader: May almighty God bless our days and deeds with peace, in the name of + the Father, and of the Son, and of the Holy Spirit.

All: **Amen.**

 CLOSING SONG

A cantor leads one of the following songs or another song that has been chosen.
"We Live A Mystery" (*Gather*)
"We Praise You" (*Gather*)
"You Will Show Me the Path of Life" (*Gather*)
"Juntos Como Hermanos" (*Flor y Canto*)

FOURTEEN

Martin Luther King, Jr.

LIVING TOGETHER AS BROTHERS AND SISTERS

A bible (lectionary), and large bowl of water is placed on a table in the center of the prayer space. The group gathers and sits near the table.

Leader: As we begin our prayer, let us listen to the words of Dr. Martin Luther King, Jr. (taken from *Where Do We Go From Here: Chaos or Community*, Abingdon Press, 1967).

The leader directs one group member to read the part listed for Reader 1.

Reader 1: "What we are seeing now is a freedom explosion, the realization of an 'idea whose time is come' . . . the deep rumbling of discontent that we hear today is the thunder of the disinherited masses, rising from dungeons of oppression to the bright hills of freedom. In one majestic chorus the rising masses are singing, in the words of our freedom song, 'Aint gonna let nobody turn us around.'"

After a brief time of silent or directed reflection, the leader directs a second group member to read the part for Reader 2.

Reader 2: ". . . today our very survival depends on our ability to stay awake, to adjust to new ideas, to remain vigilant and to face the challenge of change. The large house in which we live demands that we transform our worldwide neighborhood . . . together we must learn to live as brothers and sisters or together we will be forced to perish as fools."

OPENING SONG

Song books are distributed. A cantor leads one of the following songs or another song that has been chosen.
"I Shall Not Be Moved" (*Lead Me, Guide Me*)
"We Shall Overcome" (*Lead Me, Guide Me*)
"Anthem" (*Gather*)
"Bring Forth the Kingdom" (*Gather*)

The leader walks to the table and signs him or herself with the water and continues.

Leader: God, you created the human race and are the fountain of our renewal. As true children of the promise, enrich our lives to rejoice in justice which springs, not from our own power, but from the mystery of your love. We ask this through Christ our Lord.

All: **Amen.**

A selection of instrumental background music is played. The group members go individually to the bowl of water and sign themselves. They are seated for the scripture reading that follows.

Reader 1: A reading from the Acts of the Apostles.
Acts 10:34-38 (Lectionary, #21)

One or more group members may give reflections that pertain to the catholicity of the church and the need for acceptance among all races and genders, both in the church and in the world at large. After the reflections, the leader continues.

Leader: Let us pray.

God, we celebrate the many races and cultures among us. Please continue to bless the richness of our diversity. As we look at the faces of those gathered here, in our parish, and neighboring community, teach us to appreciate the beauty in each person. We ask this in your name.

All: **Amen.**

The group members stand, hold hands, and recite the Our Father.

 ## CLOSING SONG

A cantor leads one of the following songs or another song that has been chosen.
"Gather Us In" (*Gather*)
"Lift Ev'ry Voice and Sing" (*Lead Me, Guide Me*)
"Amémonos de Corazón" (*Flor y Canto*)
"Bendigamos al Señor" (*Flor y Canto*)

FIFTEEN

Prayer for Christian Unity

WORKING TOWARD A
COMMUNION OF LOVE

A bible (lectionary) is placed on a table in a prominent spot in the prayer space. The group members stand for the opening song and prayer.

 OPENING SONG

Song books are distributed. A cantor leads one of the following songs or another song that has been chosen.
"In Christ There Is No East or West" (*Lead Me, Guide Me*)
"Baptized in Water" (*Gather*)
"For the Healing of the Nations" (*Worship*)
"Christ is the World's Light" (*Worship*)
"Himno de la Alegría" (*Flor y Canto*)

Leader: Almighty and eternal God,
            you keep together those you have united.
            Look kindly on all who follow Jesus your Son.
            We are all consecrated to you by our common baptism;
            make us one in the fullness of faith
            and keep us one in the fellowship of love.

We ask this through our Lord Jesus Christ, your Son,
who lives and reigns with you and the Holy Spirit,
one God, for ever and ever.
(Sacramentary, Masses and Prayers for Various Needs and
Occasions, #13)

All: **Amen.**

All sit for the reading.

Reader 1:   A reading from the letter to the Ephesians.
Ephesians 4:1-6 (Lectionary, #753 or #111)

*After a brief moment of silent reflection, the leader begins a prayer
of the faithful. After the first prayer, he or she passes the book
around the circle so that other group members read the succeeding
prayers. The response to each prayer is "Lord, fill us with the
spirit of love."*

Leader: Let us pray for faith that is growing and lively, open to new
ideas, but grounded in ancient wisdom. We pray . . .

All: **Lord, fill us with the spirit of love.**

Reader 2:   Let us pray for faith that makes us willing to do as Christ
asks, that follows gladly where Christ leads, and risks
moving from narrow boundaries of comfort. We pray . . .

All: **Lord, fill us with the spirit of love.**

Reader 3:   Let us pray for faith that is strong enough to respect the
belief of others, and that does not crumble in the face of
prejudice. We pray . . .

All: **Lord, fill us with the spirit of love.**

Reader 4:   Let us pray for faith to find ways to bring the hearts of
believers together and to be open to healing divisions
among Christians. We pray . . .

All: **Lord, fill us with the spirit of love.**

Reader 5:	Let us pray that our parish community may have the strength to always bear witness to Christ's resurrection. We pray . . .
All:	**Lord, fill us with the spirit of love.**
Reader 6:	Let us pray that God will teach us to use wisely the good gifts we have been granted and that we may be led to the eternal blessings of Christ's promise.
All:	**Lord, fill us with your love.**

All stand, join hands, and recite together the Our Father.

 CLOSING SONG

A cantor leads one of the following songs or another song that has been chosen.
"We Are Many Parts" (*Gather*)
"Lead Me, Guide Me" (*Lead Me, Guide Me*)
"Where True Love and Charity are Found/Ubi Caritas (*Worship*)
"Un Pueblo Que Camina" (*Flor y Canto*)

Leader:	Lord Jesus, we ask your support for all people who believe in you. May we too share in your blessings. We pray that you bless our days and deeds in the name of + the Father, and of the Son, and of the Holy Spirit.
All:	**Amen.**

February

SIXTEEN

Lenten Promises

SEEKING A PERSONAL CONVERSION OF OUR HEARTS

A bible (lectionary), lit candle, and container of incense are placed on a table located in a prominent area of the prayer space. The group members take song books and stand near the table.

 OPENING SONG

A cantor leads one of the following songs or another song that has been chosen.
"Lead Me, Guide Me" (*Lead Me, Guide Me*)
"Tree of Life" (*Gather*)
"Gather Us In" (*Gather*)
"Here I Am Lord" (*Gather*)
"Now We Remain" (*Gather*)
"Lord When You Came/Pescador De Hombres"
(*Flor y Canto* and *Lead Me, Guide Me*)
"Perdona a Tu Pueblo" (*Flor y Canto*)

Leader: All powerful God,
            your mercy has no bounds.
            Remain with your people during this holy lenten season

and guide our ways in accord with your will.
Shelter us with your protection,
give us the light of your grace,
and help us to always seek your kingdom.
We ask this through Christ our Lord.

All: **Amen.**

Reader: A reading from the book of the prophet Ezekiel.
Ezekiel 36:23-28 (Lectionary, #422)
or
A reading from the letter to the Colossians.
Colossians 1:9-14 (Lectionary, #434)

A cantor leads the following song or another song that has been chosen as a response to the reading.

"Psalm 95, If Today You Hear His Voice" (*Gather*)

After the response to the reading, the leader continues with a prayer of intercession. The response is "Lead me, guide me, Lord."

Leader: Dear Jesus, you are the alpha and the omega, the beginning and end of life's journey. You have given your life to help us to find our way. We pray . . .

All: **Lead me, guide me, Lord.**

Leader: Many disciples who have gone before us have modeled your way. Help us to follow their example. We pray . . .

All: **Lead me, guide me, Lord.**

Leader: You guide your pilgrim church on earth through the Holy Spirit. May we seek you in all things and walk always in your love. We pray . . .

All: **Lead me, guide me, Lord.**

Leader: Our only goal is you. Grant that one day we may see you face to face in heaven. We pray . . .

All: **Lead me, guide me, Lord.**

Leader: You know our strengths and weaknesses. You know when
we sit and when we stand. Help us to always be willing to
grasp your hand and walk readily in your ways. We pray . . .

All: **Lead me, guide me, Lord.**

All stand, join hands, and recite together the Our Father.

Leader: May almighty God forgive our sins and bring us to
everlasting life in the name of + the Father, and of the Son,
and of the Holy Spirit.

All: **Amen.**

SEVENTEEN

Lenten Reconciliation

EXAMINING OUR NEED FOR GOD'S
MERCY AND COMPASSION

The lighting in the prayer space is dimmed or lighted only by candles. The group members gather outside the entrance and process slowly and silently into the room following a cross bearer who holds a cross or crucifix and a reader who holds a bible or lectionary. The procession stops at a prominently placed table, where the items are placed. While making a sign of the cross, the leader begins.

Leader: In the name of + the God who creates us, in the name of the God who is always with us, in the name of the God who saves us.

All: Amen.

Leader: Let us pray.
Lord God, your Son's passion won for us new life.
By our communal practice of penance during this lenten season, help us to a new understanding of this ultimate victory.
We ask this through Christ our Lord.

All: Amen.

Reader 1: A reading from the holy gospel according to John.
John 9:1, 6-9, 13-17, 34-38 (Lectionary, #31)

 SONG RESPONSE

After a brief period of reflective silence, song books are distributed.
A cantor leads one of the following songs or another song that has
been chosen.
"There is a Balm in Gilead" (*Lead Me, Guide Me*)
"We Walk by Faith" (*Gather*)
"Amémonos De Corazón" (*Flor y Canto*)

The group members sit in a circle of chairs. An examination of
conscience is held. A brief period of silence is observed between
each set of questions. The leader begins. He or she designates other
members of the group as readers for the following sets of questions.

Leader: Come, Holy Spirit. Help us to honestly examine our lives. Do we place our whole trust in God? Who are the false gods that we worship?

Reader 2: How generous are we with our time, money, gifts, and talents? Do we share possessions with the less fortunate or are we blinded to other people's needs by self-righteousness or judgmental attitudes?

Reader 3: How loving are we to our family members? to our fellow parishioners? to members of this group? Do our words and actions reflect the loving mission of Christ?

Reader 4: Do we take time to forgive others? Do we admit our own guilt and ask for forgiveness. How open are we to God's mercy and compassion?

The cross bearer takes the cross and brings it to the group
members one by one. Each person shows a sign of respect to the
cross (a kiss or a bow). The cross bearer holds the cross aloft as the
group members stand, hold hands, and recite the Our Father. The
leader concludes.

Leader: Let us begin our walk to healing and reconciliation by offering each other a sign of Christ's peace.

The group members share a sign of peace using this form: "Peace
be with you. And also with you."

EIGHTEEN

Lenten Reflection

TURNING OUR LIVES TOWARD GOD

A bible (lectionary) and an unlit candle are placed on a table located in a prominent place in the prayer space. The group members stand near the table for the beginning of the prayer. Song books are distributed.

Leader: We are specially chosen by God. From all eternity God has called us to be a faithful and holy people. Our response to God is to seek a life of greater holiness, of greater service, and of greater love. We gather to reflect on God's call and to pledge a stronger response to God's plan for us.

 OPENING SONG

A cantor leads one of the following songs or another song that was chosen. During the singing, one person is designated to light the candle.
"Now We Remain" (*Gather*)
"Where He Leads Me" (*Lead Me, Guide Me*)
"I Have Decided to Follow Jesus" (*Lead Me, Guide Me*)
"There Is a Balm in Gilead" (*Worship*)
"Le Conocen" (*Flor y Canto*)

All are seated for the reading.

Reader:	A reading from the book of Deuteronomy. Deuteronomy 30:15-20 (Lectionary, #221) or A reading from the book of the prophet Jeremiah. Jeremiah 17:5-10 (Lectionary, #234)
	After a brief period of reflective silence, the leader continues with the following prayer. The response is "Blessed be God forever."
Leader:	Lord, you remind us of your presence in the world. You are the same God who guided your people throughout history, and you continue to regard us with love and concern. For this, we say . . .
All:	**Blessed be God forever.**
Leader:	Lord, you have lifted from us the burden of sin and guilt. You respond to our pleas for deliverance and remain with us through our trials and conflicts. For this, we say . . .
All:	**Blessed be God forever.**
Leader:	Lord, you help us to remember the times we have neglected to listen to you and have hardened our hearts to your saving Word. Yet you relentlessly call us to yourself. For this, we say . . .
All:	**Blessed be God forever.**
Leader:	Lord, you repeat your promises to meet our needs and enrich our lives. You heal our hurts and bring us to new life. For this, we say . . .
All:	**Blessed be God forever.**
Leader:	Help us Lord, to always follow your will as we strive to serve our families, our parish, and this group. May your great love flood our lives so that they overflow and touch all whom we meet. We make this prayer in your name.
All:	**Amen.**
	The leader designates two ministers to help in making the sign of the cross on the foreheads of the group members. The minister says, "Receive with joy this sign of Christ's love." After the signing, the group members return to their seats for a brief period of silent reflection. When the leader extinguishes the candle, the prayer service ends.

March

NINETEEN

Prayer for Catechumens

BEING A WELCOMING COMMUNITY FOR ALL WHO SEEK GOD

The group members gather in a common area. A single candle is lit in the midst of the assembly. All stand. Song books are distributed.

Leader: O Lord, fill us with your Spirit.

All: **Come, Holy Spirit, fill the hearts of your faithful
and kindle in them the fire of your love.
Send forth your Spirit, O Lord,
and renew the face of the earth.**

 OPENING SONG

A cantor leads one of the following songs or another song that has been chosen.
"I Walk as a Child of the Light" (*Gather*)
"I Have Decided to Follow Jesus" (*Lead Me, Guide Me*)
"Jesus, Remember Me" (*Lead Me, Guide Me*)
"My Song Is Love Unknown" (*Worship*)
"O Sun of Justice" (*Worship*)
"Le Conocen" (*Flor y Canto*)

Leader:	God, we pray for your blessings on all your ministers gathered here. Please bless the catechumens and all those preparing for full initiation into our community during this season. Grant us the grace and guidance we need to help us remain strong and steadfast as a community of faith. We ask this through Jesus Christ, our Lord and brother.
All:	**Amen.**

The cantor leads the singing of one verse or refrain from the opening song. Following the singing, all are seated.

Reader:	A reading from the Acts of the Apostles. Acts 2:42-47 (Lectionary, #44)

The leader directs a shared reflection on the reading. He or she asks: "As a group, how do we model the Christian lifestyle?" After group members share their responses, the leader continues.

Leader:	O God, we thank you for the grace and guidance you have given us. Help us to clearly hear your voice. May we go forth to fulfill our ministry in accordance to your will. We ask this through Jesus Christ, our Lord and brother.
All:	**Amen.**

CLOSING SONG

A cantor leads one of the following songs or another song that has been chosen.
"Remember Your Love" (*Gather*)
"Take Me to the Water" (*Lead Me, Guide Me*)
"There Is One Lord" (*Worship*)

TWENTY

Springtime

RENEWING OUR LIVES IN A SEASON OF CHANGE

If possible, the group members gather near the church's baptismal font. If not, a bowl of holy water is placed on a table located in a prominent part of the prayer space. The group members stand in a circle around the font or table. Song books are distributed.

Leader: In this season of change, let us praise the Lord from whom we have rain from the heavens and abundance from the earth.

 OPENING SONG

A cantor leads one of the following songs or another song that has been chosen.
"God of Day and God of Darkness" (*Gather*)
"How Great Thou Art" (*Lead Me, Guide Me*)
"Praise God from Whom All Blessings Flow"
(*Lead Me, Guide Me*)
"Yo Tengo un Gozo" (*Flor y Canto*)

All are seated.

Reader: A reading from the book of Wisdom.
Wisdom 13:1-9 (Lectionary, #495)
or
Romans 8:18-25 (Lectionary, #480)

As a recording of reflective instrumental music is played, the group members process individually to the holy water, bless themselves, and return to their seats. After the blessings, the leader continues with the following intercessory prayer. The response is "Our souls are thirsting for the living God."

Leader: Let us pray that our minds, hearts, and souls may be converted in this season of change. For a willingness to take up the cross of Christ, we pray . . .

All: **Our souls are thirsting for the living God.**

Leader: For reconciliation between ourselves and our neighbors, we pray . . .

All: **Our souls are thirsting for the living God.**

Leader: For a willingness to follow the model of Mary and the saints, we pray . . .

All: **Our souls are thirsting for the living God.**

Leader: For success of this group's special ministry, we pray . . .

All: **Our souls are thirsting for the living God.**

Leader: For the people of *NAME OF PARISH* whom we serve, we pray . . .

All: **Our souls are thirsting for the living God.**

Leader: Loving Creator of the universe,
you have given us great responsibilities
as co-creators with you.
Direct us in using all created things with care
and sharing your gifts with those in need.
We pray this in Jesus' name.

All: **Amen.**

The group members share a sign of peace using this form: "Peace be with you. And also with you."

# CLOSING SONG

A cantor leads one of the following songs or another song that has been chosen.
"O Healing River" (*Gather*)
"Come to the Water" (*Gather*)
"Gracias Señor" (*Flor y Canto*)

TWENTY ~ ONE

Easter

CELEBRATING CHRIST'S RESURRECTION

A lit paschal candle is placed in the center of the room. Chairs are arranged in a circle around the candle. The group members gather and stand near the chairs.

OPENING SONG

Song books are distributed. A cantor leads one of the following songs or another song that has been chosen.
"The Lord is My Light" (*Gather*)
"We Have Been Told" (*Gather*)
"Spirit of the Living God" (*Lead Me, Guide Me*)
"Hallelujah Song" (*Lead Me, Guide Me*)
"The Strife is O'er" (*Worship*)
"Resucitó" (*Flor y Canto*)

The group members make a sign of the cross. The leader continues.

Leader: God of glory, the eyes of all turn to you as we celebrate
           Christ's victory over sin and death and the joy of new life.
           Help those gathered here in your presence be created anew
           as a community of faith, rooted in the love of Christ.
           We ask this in Jesus' name.

All:	**Amen.**

All are seated.

Reader 1:	A reading from the Acts of the Apostles. Acts 4:8-12 (Lectionary, #51)

The leader directs a shared reflection on the reading. He or she asks: "How is Jesus the foundation of our common ministry?" After all have had a chance to share, a second reader leads the intercessory prayer. The response is "Lord, hear our prayer."

Reader 2:	For the ability to clearly recognize the new life offered to us by Christ, let us pray . . .
All:	**Lord, hear our prayer.**
Reader 2:	For acceptance of Christ's call to give to those who hunger and thirst for justice, let us pray . . .
All:	**Lord, hear our prayer.**
Reader 2:	For those who were initiated into our community of faith during this Easter season, let us pray . . .
All:	**Lord, hear our prayer.**
Reader 2:	For our own special intentions as spoken now.

The group members share their individual intentions. When all have shared, the leader continues.

Leader:	Loving God, hear our prayers. May our baptism into one faith bring joy to the world. We ask this in the name of Jesus Christ our Lord.
All:	**Amen.**

CLOSING SONG

A cantor leads one of the following songs or another song that has been chosen.
"Sing A New Song" (*Gather*)

"Sign Me Up" (*Lead Me, Guide Me*)
"I Know That My Redeemer Lives" (*Lead Me, Guide Me*)
"Christ the Lord Is Risen Today" (*Worship*)
"Tú Reinarás" (*Flor y Canto*)

April

TWENTY ~ TWO

Jesus Is Risen!

REJOICING IN THE SEASON OF NEW LIFE

A bible (lectionary), lit candle, and a bowl of water is placed on a table located in a prominent location in the prayer space. The group members take a songbook and gather near the table.

 OPENING SONG

A cantor leads one of the following songs or another song that has been chosen.
"Easter Alleluia" (*Gather*)
"Spirit of the Living God" (*Lead Me, Guide Me*)
"Christ the Lord Is Risen Today" (*Worship*)
"Amor Es Vida" (*Flor y Canto*)

Leader: God, our Creator,
            through the miracle of Easter, we are reborn to new life.
            As we meditate on this glorious truth,
            we ask that we might live every day
            in reflection of the resurrection.
            We ask this through Christ our Lord and Savior.

All: **Amen.**

Reader:	A reading from the first letter of Peter. 1 Peter 1:3-9 (Lectionary, #44)
	The leader directs a shared reflection on the reading. He or she asks: "How would you describe the great joy that Christ has won for you by his resurrection? How does this joy translate to your ministry?" After the sharing, the leader continues.
Leader:	Let us make a profession of faith. Do you believe in God, the Father almighty, creator of heaven and earth?
All:	**I do.**
Leader:	Do you believe in Jesus Christ, his only Son, our Lord, who was born of the Virgin Mary, was crucified, died, and was buried, rose from the dead, and is now seated at the right hand of the Father?
All:	**I do.**
Leader:	Do you believe in the Holy Spirit, the holy catholic church, the communion of saints, the forgiveness of sins, the resurrection of the body, and life everlasting?
All:	**I do.**
Leader:	This is our faith. This is the faith of the church. We are proud to profess it, in Christ Jesus our Lord.
All:	**Amen.**
	The leader leads a procession of group members to the bowl of water, dipping his or her hand in the water and making a sign of the cross. When all have finished, the leader continues.
Leader:	O God, through our baptism we are made one in faith and heirs to a salvation filled with joy. We praise and thank you for our rebirth in Christ as we stand, join hands, and pray:

Our Father, who art in heaven. . . .
Let us offer each other a sign of peace.

The group members share a sign of peace using this form: "Peace be with you. And also with you."

 CLOSING SONG

A cantor leads one of the following songs or another song that has been chosen.
"Sing Alleluia" (*Glory and Praise 3*)
"Hallelujah Song" (*Lead Me, Guide Me*)
"Resucitó" (*Flor y Canto*)

TWENTY ~ THREE

Easter Season

SHEPHERDING OUR NEW LIFE IN FAITH

A lit paschal candle is in the center of the prayer space. Nearby, a bible (lectionary) and a bowl of water that can be easily lifted are placed on a table. The group members gather with songbooks near the candle and table. Holding the bowl of water aloft, the leader begins.

Leader: Loving God, our one, true shepherd.
During this Easter season we recall the new life won for us through the actions of your Son.
Through baptism, we are united with him.
May this water remind us of our faith commitment.
We ask this in your name.

All: **Amen.**

 OPENING SONG

The leader blesses himself or herself with the water and passes the bowl to a next person. As the blessing takes place, a cantor leads one of the following songs or another song that has been chosen.
"We Will Rise Again" (*Gather*)
"The Lord Is My Shepherd" (*Lead Me, Guide Me*)
"The Lord, the Lord, the Lord Is My Shepherd" (*Worship*)

All are seated.

Reader 1:	A reading from the holy gospel according to John. John 10:11-16 (Lectionary, #724)

The leader directs a shared reflection on the reading. He or she asks: "How does Jesus model the good shepherd for you? How are you a good shepherd to others in your family? in this group? in the parish?" After the sharing, a second reader continues with the following intercessory prayer. The response is "Lord, hear our prayer."

Reader 2:	For an Easter season filled with hopefulness and commitment to live our Christian faith anew, we pray . . .

All: **Lord, hear our prayer.**

Reader 2:	For the ability to separate ourselves from false shepherds and from sins of hatred and divisiveness, we pray . . .

All: **Lord, hear our prayer.**

Reader 2:	For the continuing centering of this group and our entire parish community in the new life offered by Jesus' resurrection, we pray . . .

All: **Lord, hear our prayer.**

Reader 2:	For the courage to welcome the stranger and the strength to heal the brokenhearted, we pray . . .

All: **Lord, hear our prayer.**

Reader 2:	For our own special intentions as spoken now.

The group members share their individual intentions. When all have shared, the leader continues.

Leader:	Christ is risen! Alleluia! Alleluia!

All: **Alleluia! Alleluia!**

Leader:	Let us offer each other a sign of Christ's peace.

The group members share a sign of peace using this form: "Peace be with you. And also with you."

CLOSING SONG

A cantor leads one of the following songs or another song that has been chosen.

"Baptized in Water" (*Gather*)

"Gift of Finest Wheat" (*Lead Me, Guide Me*)

"El Peregrino de Emaús" (*Flor y Canto*)

TWENTY FOUR

Prayer for Neophytes

OFFERING SUPPORT FOR NEWLY BAPTIZED MEMBERS OF OUR COMMUNITY

A bible (lectionary) and lit candle are placed on a table located in a prominent place in the prayer space. The group members stand near a circle of chairs placed around the table to begin the prayer.

 OPENING SONG

Song books are distributed. A cantor leads one of the following songs or another song that has been chosen.
"I Have Loved You" (*Gather*)
"I've Got the Joy, Joy, Joy" (*Lead Me, Guide Me*)
"I Know That My Redeemer Lives" (*Worship*)
"This Is the Spirit's Entry Now" (*Worship*)
"Tu Palabra Me Da Vida" (*Flor y Canto*)

Leader: God, you call us to be one in faith and community.
Give us the strength to serve you with all our hearts
and to work together with unselfish love.
We ask this through Christ our Lord.

All: **Amen.**

All are seated.

Reader 1:	A reading from the holy gospel according to John. John 17:1-11a (Lectionary, #60)

The leader directs a period of sharing in which each group member suggests ways the group can offer support to the neophytes of the parish. An optional idea is to invite the neophytes to this meeting and have the group members share personal anecdotes and remembrances about parish life. Following the sharing, a second reader leads a prayer for the neophytes. The response is "Lord, hear our prayer."

Reader 2:	For strength and courage for the neophytes as they continue in their new life, we pray . . .

All: **Lord, hear our prayer.**

Reader 2:	For our group, that we may offer ongoing support to the neophytes in all their efforts, we pray . . .

All: **Lord, hear our prayer.**

Reader 2:	For our parish, that we may learn from the neophytes to see our community with the new eyes of faith, we pray . . .

All: **Lord, hear our prayer.**

After the intercessory prayer, the leader calls all to stand, join hands, and recite the Our Father.

 CLOSING SONG

A cantor leads one of the following songs or another song that has been chosen.
"Good Christians All" (*Gather*)
"Let All That is Within Me Cry Holy" (*Lead Me, Guide Me*)
"Glorious in Majesty" (*Worship*)

May

TWENTY FIVE

HONORING THE MOTHER OF GOD

A bible (lectionary) and lit candle are placed on a table or podium located in a prominent place in the prayer space. The group members stand to begin the prayer.

Leader: Let us pray in the name of Jesus,
born of Mary, a child of God.

There is a brief moment of silence for personal prayer

Father,
you prepared the heart of the Virgin Mary
to be a fitting home for your Holy Spirit.
By her prayers
may we become a more worthy temple of your glory.
Grant this through our Lord Jesus Christ, your Son,
who lives and reigns with you and the Holy Spirit,
one God, for ever and ever.
(Sacramentary, Proper of Saints, Immaculate Heart of Mary)

All: **Amen.**

 OPENING SONG

Song books are distributed. A cantor leads one of the following songs or another song that has been chosen.
"Canticle of Mary—My Soul Gives Glory" (*Gather*)
"Sing of Mary, Pure and Lowly" (*Lead Me, Guide Me*)

Reader 1: A reading from the holy gospel according to Luke.
Luke 1:46-56 (Lectionary, #199)

All are seated. The leader directs a period of shared reflection. He or she asks: "When was a time you emptied yourself to follow God's will? What risks were associated with your actions? How did your trusting faith bring you new life?" After everyone has shared, a recording of instrumental music is played softly as a second reader reads the following meditation.

Reader 2: We worship God as Mother and Father,
the ground of our being,
the source of our life,
the Spirit who sets us free.
In memory of all mothers
who have sung praise to God
before their children were born
we join to honor the faithfulness of Mary
and the Spirit of God in our midst.
To worship is to open our beings
to the power of God's truth and love.
To worship is to heighten our awareness
of the core of our existence,
the meaning of life.
We learn the meaning of worship through
the example of Mary, God's lowly handmaid,
who played such a vital role in our salvation.
Let us celebrate with joy
in the hope that our awareness and openness
will bear the fruit of increased union
with God's Spirit in each of us.

After the meditation, the leader calls all to stand and recite together a Hail Mary.

 CLOSING SONG

A cantor leads one of the following songs or another song that has been chosen.
"Immaculate Mary" (*Worship*)
"Sing We of the Blessed Mother" (*Worship*)
"O María, Madre Mía" (*Flor y Canto*)

TWENTY SIX

Pentecost

SHARING THE GIFTS OF THE SPIRIT

A lit candle—preferably the paschal candle—is located in a prominent area of the prayer space. A bible (lectionary) and flask of scented oil for anointing is placed on a nearby table. The group members pick up a song book and stand for the beginning of the prayer.

 OPENING SONG

A cantor leads one of the following songs or another song that has been chosen.
"Veni Sancte Spiritus" (*Gather*)
"Ye Watchers and Ye Holy Ones" (*Worship*)

Leader: Come, Holy Spirit.
Inspire our prayer and be with us
at this meeting and in all times and all ways.

There is a brief moment of silence for personal prayer.

The days since Easter have revealed the depth of your love for us.

See your people gathered in prayer,
open to receive the flame of your inspiration.
May you come to rest in our hearts
and disperse the divisions of word and action.
With one voice we praise your name in thanksgiving.
We pray in the name of the most Blessed Trinity.

All: **Amen.**

Reader 1:   A reading from the Acts of the Apostles.
Acts 2:1-11 (Lectionary, #64)

After a brief time of silent reflection, the leader continues.

Leader: At confirmation, we are sealed with the Holy Spirit
to be more like Christ and a more perfect member of his
church. Please accept this anointing as a sign of this
commitment.

*The group members process in pairs to the table with oil. Each
person anoints the hands of the other person using these or similar
words: "Let your hands be strong in the service of God's reign."
After the anointing, the leader continues.*

Leader: God, through Jesus Christ, you have freed us from all sin
and given us new birth by water and the Holy Spirit.
As Christ was anointed priest, prophet, and king,
so may we always take our place
as a special member of Christ's body, the church.
We make this prayer in your name.

All: **Amen.**

*A second reader leads an intercessory prayer. The response is
"Come, Holy Spirit."*

Reader 2:   For the gift of fortitude to persevere in all the tasks we face
as a group, we pray . . .

All: **Come, Holy Spirit.**

Reader 2:   For the gift of understanding to respond kindly to the needs
of others, we pray . . .

All: **Come, Holy Spirit.**

Reader 2: For the gift of counsel to offer advice when asked and accept advice when needed, we pray . . .

All: **Come, Holy Spirit.**

Reader 2: For the gift of knowledge to accept the truth of Christ's teachings, we pray . . .

All: **Come, Holy Spirit.**

Reader 2: For the gift of wisdom to share the lessons of our experience for the betterment of our group's mission, we pray . . .

All: **Come, Holy Spirit.**

Reader 2: For the gift of piety to accept all of our gifts from the fountain of all holiness, we pray . . .

All: **Come, Holy Spirit.**

Reader 2: For the gift of awe and respect to remain ever mindful of God's care for us, we pray . . .

All: **Come, Holy Spirit.**

After the intercessory prayer, the leader calls all to stand, join hands, and recite the Our Father.

 CLOSING SONG

A cantor leads one of the following songs or another song that has been chosen.
"Sing a New Song" (*Gather*)
"Spirit Song" (*Lead Me, Guide Me*)
"Pueblo Libre" (*Flor y Canto*)

TWENTY SEVEN

Memorial Day

REMEMBERING OUR LOVED ONES

A bible (lectionary), sand in a wide, fireproof container, and unlit tapers (not in the sand) are on a table placed in a prominent location in the prayer space. A lit paschal candle stands nearby. The group members stand in this area for the beginning of the prayer.

 OPENING SONG

Song books are distributed. A cantor leads one of the following songs or another song that has been chosen.
"Be Not Afraid" (*Gather*)
"Battle Hymn of the Republic" (*Lead Me, Guide Me*)
"Lift Ev'ry Voice and Sing" (*Lead Me, Guide Me*)

Leader: God who holds us tenderly, we keep the memorial of those who have died in service of our country.

A brief period of silence is observed.

Give these brothers and sisters the joy of your love in the company of all the saints. We ask this in the name of Jesus Christ, our brother and Lord.

All: **Amen.**

All are seated.

Reader: A reading from the letter to the Romans.
Romans 8:14-23 (Lectionary, #790)

The leader directs a period of shared reflection. The discussion is focused on remembrances of family members who have served their country, examples of heroes from their own country and other countries who have died in the service of truth, and their own understandings of the meaning of freedom. At the end of the discussion, the leader continues.

Leader: Please take this opportunity to pray for a friend or family member who has died. Come forward, one at a time, and take a taper. As you light it from the paschal candle, you may pray a brief prayer aloud using these or similar words, "Give _NAME_ eternal rest, O Lord." We will all respond with, "And may your light shine on her (him) forever." Or, you may pray in silence. Then place the lit candle in the box of sand.

After all have lit candles and prayed, the leader asks all to stand, hold hands, and pray together the Our Father.

 CLOSING SONG

A cantor leads one of the following songs or another song that has been chosen.
"God of Day and God of Darkness" (*Gather*)
"When Charity and Love Prevail" (*Gather*)
"O God of Every Nation" (*Worship*)
"Let There Be Light" (*Worship*)
"Tú Reinarás" (*Flor y Canto*)

June

TWENTY EIGHT

God's Justice

FILLING THE HEARTS OF
GOD'S PEOPLE WITH LOVE

*A bible (lectionary), lit candle, and unlit tapers with wax holders
are placed on a center table located in a prominent place in the
prayer space. The group members take a song book and stand near
the table for the beginning of the prayer.*

OPENING SONG

*A cantor leads one of the following songs or another song that has
been chosen.*
"Anthem" (*Gather*)
"Bring Forth the Kingdom" (*Gather*)
"In Christ There is No East or West" (*Worship*)
"I Shall Not Be Moved" (*Lead Me, Guide Me*)

Leader: Father,
you have given all peoples one common origin,
and your will is to gather them as one family in yourself.
Fill the hearts of all with the fire of your love
and the desire to ensure justice for all their brothers
    and sisters.
By sharing the good things you give us

may we secure justice and equality for every human being,
an end to all division,
and a human society built on love and peace.
We ask this through our Lord Jesus Christ, your Son,
who lives and reigns with you and the Holy Spirit,
one God, for ever and ever.
(Sacramentary, Masses and Prayers for Various Needs and
Occasions, #21)

All: **Amen.**

*The group members replace their songbooks and take up unlit
tapers and wax holders. All are seated in a circle of chairs.*

Reader 1:   A reading from the book of the prophet Isaiah.
Isaiah 32:15-20 (Lectionary, #831)
or
Isaiah 9:1-6 (Lectionary, #831)

*After a brief period of reflective silence, the leader designates four
separate readers at equidistant intervals around the circle. Reader
2 lights his or her candle and begins with the following psalm. The
response to each passage is "The poor shall eat and have their fill."*

Reader 2:   I will proclaim your name to my brothers and sisters;
In the midst of the assembly I will praise you:
"You who fear God, praise God;
all your descendants of Jacob, give glory to God."

All: **The poor shall eat and have their fill.**

*Reader 2 lights his or her taper from the large candle and passes
the light to the next person in the direction of Reader 3. All
candles are lit to the person just prior to Reader 3. Reader 3
continues.*

Reader 3:   So by your gift I will utter praise in the vast assembly;
I will fulfill my vows before those who fear God.
The lowly shall eat their fill;
they who seek God shall praise God.

All: **The poor shall eat and have their fill.**

Reader 3 lights his or her taper from the large candle and passes the light to the next person in the direction of Reader 4. All candles are lit to the person just prior to Reader 4. Reader 4 continues.

Reader 4:   All the ends of the earth
shall remember and turn to God;
All families of the nations
shall bow before God.

All: **The poor shall eat and have their fill.**

Reader 4 lights his or her taper from the large candle and passes the light to the next person in the direction of Reader 5. All candles in the circle are lit. Reader 5 continues.

Reader 5:   And to God my soul shall live;
my descendants shall serve God.
Let the coming generation be told
that they may proclaim to a people yet to be born
the justice God has shown.

All: **The poor shall eat and have their fill.**

One or more group members are invited to share a reflection on the peace and justice efforts of the group and parish as a whole. After the reflections, the leader continues with an intercessory prayer. The response is "Lord, hear our prayer."

Leader: In humility, let us ask for God's mercy. For the willingness to make peace and prevent war, we pray . . .

All: **Lord, hear our prayer.**

Leader: For a spirit of wisdom and understanding, we pray . . .

All: **Lord, hear our prayer.**

Leader: For the courage to make changes and the serenity to accept truth, we pray . . .

All: **Lord, hear our prayer.**

Leader:	For the forgiveness of our sins and for the gift to forgive others who have hurt us, we pray . . .
All:	**Lord, hear our prayer.**
Leader:	God of life, true light of the world, you guide humankind to salvation. Give us the courage, strength, and grace to build a world of justice and peace. We ask this through Christ our Lord.
All:	**Amen.**

 CLOSING SONG

A cantor leads one of the following songs or another song that has been chosen.
"The Harvest of Justice" (*Gather*)
"For the Healing of the Nations" (*Worship*)
"We Shall Overcome" (*Lead Me, Guide Me*)
"Un Mandamiento Nuevo" (*Flor y Canto*)

TWENTY NINE

Summer

DREAMING OF TIME ETERNAL

The group members gather outside, preferably in a garden setting. If this is not possible, indoor decorations should include summer flowers and fruits. All stand for the beginning of the prayer. Song books are distributed.

Leader: God of fruitfulness,
we celebrate your gift of life
in this season of fresh rains and warm air.
Help us to grow in the truth of your Word during
these summer months.
Hear us, God, through Jesus Christ our Lord.

All: **Amen.**

OPENING SONG

A cantor leads one of the following songs or another song that has been chosen.
"I Have Loved You" (*Gather*)
"Joyous Light of Heavenly Glory" (*Gather*)
"Free at Last" (*Lead Me, Guide Me*)
"Good News" (*Lead Me, Guide Me*)
"De Colores" (*Flor y Canto*)

All are seated.

Reader 1:   A reading from the book of the prophet Isaiah.
              Isaiah 55:6-11 (Lectionary, #886)

              The leader directs a period of shared reflection. He or she asks:
              "How have you witnessed God's presence in our group and in our
              parish during the course of this past year?" After all have had a
              chance to share, Reader 2 leads the following intercessory prayer.
              The response is "Lord, hear our prayer."

Reader 2:   Let us pray. That the peacefulness of summer weather may
              be translated to peace with God, neighbor, and self,
              we pray . . .

All: **Lord, hear our prayer.**

Reader 2:   For safety of family, friends, and parishioners during this
              season of travel, we pray . . .

All: **Lord, hear our prayer.**

Reader 2:   For friendly and cooperative interaction between
              humankind and the natural environment, we pray . . .

All: **Lord, hear our prayer.**

              The group members are invited to add their own personal
              petitions. After the intercessory prayer, the leader calls all to
              stand, join hands, and recite the Our Father. The leader continues.

Leader: Let us offer each other a sign of peace.

              The group members share a sign of peace using this form: "Peace
              be with you. And also with you."

CLOSING SONG

A cantor leads one of the following songs or another song that has been chosen.

"In Praise of His Name" (*Gather*)

"Jesus, Joy of Man's Desiring" (*Lead Me, Guide Me*)

"We Walk by Faith" (*Worship*)

"For the Beauty of the Earth" (*Worship*)

"In Praise of His Name" (*Worship*)

THIRTY

End of the Year

THANKING GOD FOR OUR TIME TOGETHER

A bible (lectionary), a lit candle, and samples of the minutes for several of the group's meetings are arranged on a table located in a prominent area of the prayer space. The group members stand near the table for the beginning of the prayer. Song books are distributed.

Leader: My friends, as we conclude this part of our service for this group and for *NAME OR PARISH*, let us a share a prayer of thanks.

Dear God,
you made us and we belong to you.
We are yours both by nature and grace.
We thank you with our words, actions, and thoughts
for this time we have shared together.
Blessed be your name,
Creator, Savior, and Spirit, now and for ever.

All: **Amen.**

 OPENING SONG

A cantor leads one of the following songs or another song that has been chosen.
"Glory and Praise to Our God" (*Gather*)
"Here I Am, Lord" (*Gather*)
"God Send Us His Spirit" (*Lead Me, Guide Me*)
"Thanks Be to God" (*Worship*)
"Demos Gracias al Señor" (*Flor y Canto*)

All are seated.

Reader: A reading from the letter to the Colossians. Colossians 3:12-17 (Lectionary, #440)

The leader directs a shared reflection on the reading in relationship to the major themes covered in the course of the group's action over the past year. Volunteers are called on to share special moments of God's grace, appreciation to group members who may be leaving, and thankfulness for the work that was accomplished. After the sharing, all stand. The leader continues with the following intercessory prayer. The response is "Lord, hear the prayers of your people."

Leader: God who calls us, we pray for all people, that they may be responsive to your word . . .

All: **Lord, hear the prayers of your people.**

Leader: God who heals broken hearts, we pray for peace and harmony in a world filled with hate and violence . . .

All: **Lord, hear the prayers of your people**.

Leader: God who saves, we pray in thanksgiving for ourselves and our parish community, that we may always be a living sign of your presence . . .

All: **Lord, hear the prayers of your people.**

The group members are invited to add their own personal petitions. After the intercessory prayer, the leader calls all to stand, join hands, and recite the Our Father. The leader continues.

Leader: Let us offer each other a sign of peace.

The group members share a sign of peace using this form: "Peace be with you. And also with you."

 CLOSING SONG

A cantor leads one of the following songs or another song that has been chosen.
"Canticle of the Sun" (*Gather*)
"We Praise You, O Lord" (*Gather*)
"Spirit Song" (*Lead Me, Guide Me*)
"Praise, My Soul, the King of Heaven" (*Worship*)
"Day Is Done" (*Worship*)